11·00

1 o'clock

12·00

12 o'clock

13·00

1 o'clock

17·00

5 o'clock

18·00

6 o'clock

19·00

7 o'clock

Learning Points

The idea of time is a difficult one for young children but they see how important clocks are to us and are very keen to know what they 'say'. This colourful book with detailed pictures goes through a child's day from getting up to going to bed. Each of the familiar events is related to the time on a clock face.

- Talk about the pictures together. What are the important landmarks in your child's day – and what time do they happen?

- Focus on the hours first of all, using a clock with a dial and hands.

- Before you talk about half hours, make sure your child understands what half means. Use the word when you talk together and cut apples, cakes, sandwiches into halves.

- Using this book to help you, make your own 'family time book' with a clock on each page. Encourage your child to draw appropriate pictures.

Digital faces are included as children will meet them in their daily lives.

Produced exclusively for
ASDA Stores Ltd
Great Wilson Street
Leeds LS11 5AD
by Ladybird Books Ltd
27 Wrights Lane London
W8 5TZ

©Ladybird Books Ltd

telling the time

by Lynne Bradbury
illustrated by Lynn Breeze

ASDA
play and learn

daytime

night-time

morning

afternoon

evening

 It is 8 o'clock
in the morning.

Some people are
getting up.

Some people are
eating their breakfast.

At 9 o'clock
Mummy is working,
Daddy is working.

It is
10 o'clock.

Everyone is busy.

What are they doing?

It is
11 o'clock.

The children are
having a drink.

Then they go out to play.

At 11 o'clock
grown-ups have a
drink too.

It is
12 o'clock.

12 o'clock is the
end of the morning.

12 o'clock is the middle of the day.

At 12 o'clock
the children
are having
a meal.

Some are at home.

Some are at school.

 It is 1 o'clock
in the
afternoon.

Lots of people have
a meal at 1 o'clock.

People eat
different things.

It is
2 o'clock.

What are these
children doing?

It is
3 o'clock.

Lots of people
like a cup of
tea at 3 o'clock.

It is
4 o'clock.

The children are
coming home
from school.

They are hungry.

At 4 o'clock the children sometimes watch television...

or play with their
toys.

It is
5 o'clock.

Mummy is busy.
She is cooking.

It is
6 o'clock.

These people are going home from work.

At 6 o'clock Daddy is home.

It is
7 o'clock.

How do the
children get ready
for bedtime?

At 7 o'clock,
when the
children are
ready, it is
time for a story.

It is
8 o'clock.

The children are
asleep.

At 8 o'clock
Mummy is going out.
Daddy is watching
television.